ARCHITECTURE CAREER GUIDE

BEGINNER'S GUIDE: HOW TO BECOME AN ARCHITECT

RYAN HANSANUWAT

CHAPTER 1
INTRODUCTION TO ARCHITECTURE

CHAPTER 2
ARCHITECTURE AS A CAREER

CHAPTER 3
SKILLS NEEDED TO BE AN ARCHITECT

CHAPTER 4
ARCHITECTURE EDUCATION

CHAPTER 5
LICENSING

CHAPTER 6
LICENSING WITHOUT A DEGREE

CHAPTER 7
CONCLUSION

.

WHO IS THIS BOOK FOR?

This book is intended for anybody who is interested in pursuing a career in architecture. It is written in a manner that is accessible to anybody regardless of interest or level, but is intended for those who are new to architecture. It is for someone who might be:

-Considering careers after high-school

-Considering switching majors in college

-Considering switching careers

-Just starting out in architecture

This beginner's guide will give you insight into whether architecture is right for you and what you need to be a successful Architect.

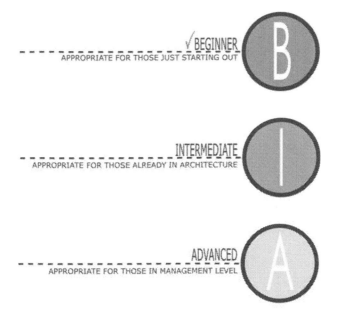

√ BEGINNER **B**
APPROPRIATE FOR THOSE JUST STARTING OUT

INTERMEDIATE **I**
APPROPRIATE FOR THOSE ALREADY IN ARCHITECTURE

ADVANCED **A**
APPROPRIATE FOR THOSE IN MANAGEMENT LEVEL

ABOUT THE AUTHOR

I wrote this book to help you become a successful Architect. I went through it recently and have learned a lot along the way. It is a long road with a lot of confusing twists and turns and I wished I had something like this to guide me through it and keep me on track. The purpose of this guide is intended to do just that...guide you. It is based on my personal experience, and written under the assumption that you want to achieve similar results. Although our paths may differ at some points, the end goal is the same, to become a successful Architect.

My name is Ryan Hansanuwat and I am a Registered/Licensed Architect in two states, I hold an NCARB certificate, a LEED Accreditation, a professional Bachelor of Architecture degree and a Master of Building Science degree. I am a Vice President of a firm focusing on Architecture and Interior Design.

I started out in a career, not related to Architecture at all. I was going to school to be an accountant and focused my life around that. Then one day I woke up and realized I didn't want to be an accountant anymore. There is nothing wrong with that career; I just yearned for more creative endeavors.

I soon enrolled in an architecture class at my community college, continued on to a undergraduate program at a university, and followed that with my Master's degree. I soon completed my work experience and the Internship Development Program during this time and started my registration exams. One year later I completed the tests and was officially a licensed Architect. I soon moved jobs (and states) and started moving my way up in the firm. Within two years at the new firm I was made Vice President and finally got there.

I was able to complete all of this in a little over a decade of work, school and personal experience by following the information detailed in this book, and hopefully you could experience similar results. I wish you luck and hope that this guide is of some service to you. If it is helpful please let me know ryan@architecturecareerguide.com

PREFACE

Becoming an Architect has been a journey for me and this is something I don't always like to talk about because I don't like comparing the paths people take. We are all different and have different things we deal with in life, so no two paths will be the same. Anyways, I will tell you how I got here in hopes that it might help somebody else and the path they are taking.

Let's just get this out of the way...I am technically a high school dropout. I'm not proud of that fact, but there were many reasons why it happened. I wasn't a bad kid in school, I didn't get bad grades, in fact I was on track to graduate early, but personal reasons led me to stop going to school. I started working after I dropped out and eventually went back to get my GED, but the fact still remains that I did not graduate high school. This is probably the reason that when I decided what I was going to do with my life, I went full speed into it. I decided that the job I had didn't have a future, so I went back to school, but I still floated around for a while not knowing what I wanted to do.

When you ask most Architects when they knew they wanted to be an Architect, a lot of times they will tell you they have known since they were 5 years old, but that wasn't the case with me. At 5 years old, I knew for sure I wanted to be a veterinarian. I had a lot of animals, from fish to horses, and I wanted nothing more than to be able to take care of them. That was until I got older and realized taking care of them also meant seeing them in pain, and that just wasn't for me. During high school, I was sure I was going to be in some sort of business related occupation. My Dad was an accountant, my Aunts and Uncles were in finance or real estate, so why not? I took many business courses, until one day I woke up and realized that I didn't want to work with just numbers my whole life. I did like the fact

7

that there was always an answer and problems could be solved through math, but I was yearning for something more, something "artistic". I signed up for an Introduction to Architecture class at the local community college and haven't turned back since. I was well into my 20's when I realized I wanted to be an Architect.

After taking a few drafting courses at junior college, I applied for Architecture school and got flat out rejected. I proceeded to take more classes, got a job as an intern, worked on my portfolio and tried again the next year. I not only got into school, but had advanced placement and started out in 2nd year. I was excited about this, since in my mind, I took too long to find what I wanted to do and wasted that time. I was a little older than most applicants and was close to giving up, thinking that maybe I couldn't compete with the high school kids. This couldn't be farther from the truth, because in reality I was only a couple of years older than most of the students and in fact brought my experience with me that they may not have had. By the time I started school I was already married and had rent and bills to pay, but I came in eager and ready to learn.

Because I had a family and bills to pay, I continued to work full-time in architecture while doing a full load of architecture classes. I was able to take the knowledge that I learned at work-work and apply it to my school-work, and vice-versa. Somewhere in the middle of undergrad my son was born, and my life changed instantly. I dedicated myself to getting the most I could from school and work, knowing that I had to succeed because I had an even bigger family relying on me. Around this time the USGBC and LEED started becoming very popular, so between work, school and family, I studied for the exam. I took study guides with me everywhere I went. I studied on lunch breaks, weekends, even vacations, and because of that I passed easily. I got my first set of letters behind my name.

I worked extra hard at school and went out of my way to learn as much as I can, in Architecture and in other areas. I graduated with honors from undergrad with a professional architecture degree, but yearned for a more specialized education. I applied to four universities and was rejected by two, wait-listed by one and thankfully was accepted to my first choice. I entered USC's Building Science program and was fortunate to also have been offered a scholarship, but I still continued working because, you know, bills. By this time I was almost complete with my internship hours due to all the years of working while in school so I also started taking my Architectural Registration Exam's at that time. I had my second child while in grad school and suddenly had another person to be accountable for. So between working full-time, a full load at grad school, two kids plus a 2-hour commute, I still completed my IDP and took all of my ARE's. I still remember the day I graduated. May 14th we had commencement and I had a party with my family and friends. I had taken my last ARE a few months prior and decided to check the mail. I received my last pass letter for the ARE's the same day I finished grad school. That really was a graduation day, finished with school and finished with ARE's. After graduation I moved my family to Texas, landed a good job and kept working my way up, learning all I could along the way.

I say all of this not to brag about all that I have done, but to hopefully inspire you. Getting through architecture school is hard. Landing (and keeping) a job is hard. Finishing IDP is hard. Caring for a family is hard. Passing your ARE's is hard. I may be a glutton for punishment, but I was able to do all of these things, and all at the same time. In the span of six years, I got a good job in architecture, received two degrees, raised a family, completed IDP and passed all of my exams, and only because I worked hard and never stopped learning (and had an incredibly supportive wife).

This is also what inspired me to start the Architecture Career Guide website, to give others the tools needed to accomplish their goals as well. The wonderful feedback has led me to also write this book. My hope is that with the information provided within, anybody who wants to become an Architect will have the direction they need. For those just getting started, or for those in the middle of it, the information you need to get you along the right path are contained within. Best of luck

CHAPTER 1
INTRODUCTION TO ARCHITECTURE

WHAT IS ARCHITECTURE?

Architecture, at its core, is a noun that describes any built structure around us, and by that definition it can be anything from a skyscraper to a dog house. But beyond the dictionary term, architecture can be so much more. It can be the connection between human needs and the physical manifestation of those needs. People need shelter, and Architects design the houses that meet that need. A religious group needs a place to worship, architecture provides them that opportunity. Architecture is the relationship between construction materials and their use in meeting the users needs.

In addition to the physical manifestations, architecture can also exhibit non-physical characteristics. Good architecture doesn't just take into account construction, but also aspects such as the light in the space, the texture of materials, and the relationship of spaces to each other. In a sense, true architecture is more about designing what is not seen, than what is actually there. Architecture is both art and science at the same time, which makes it extremely interesting.

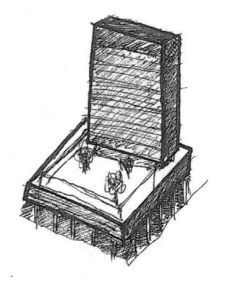

WHAT DOES AN ARCHITECT DO?

With the definition of what architecture is in mind, what exactly does an Architect do then? As a basic overview, Architects create the designs for buildings and put together the drawings necessary for the building to get built. They are primarily responsible for meeting with the person or group that wants to build something, coming up with a design that meets their needs and figuring out how to actually build the design.

The buildings that Architects design can range from simple structures like park pavilions, restroom buildings and shade structures all the way up to multilevel skyscrapers. Architects are also involved in designing many houses; in fact, the house you live in now was probably designed by an Architect. If you want to visually see the influence an Architect can have on the world, you just need to look around your neighborhood, community, or city to see many buildings that were designed by Architects.

"So Architects don't actually build the buildings?" Not usually. There are times when an Architect might also be the builder, but the typical role in the last century is that the Architect specializes in the area of design, while working together with a builder who specializes in the construction of the building. This specialization in design means that the Architect can focus on important aspects like aesthetics, function of the spaces, usability of the spaces and other critical items.

Beyond the actual design of the buildings and the creation of the building plans, Architects also take on many other important roles such as helping the owner figure out what they want in the building (programming), working with consultants such as civil, structural, mechanical, electrical, and plumbing engineers to make sure the design will work and is a comfortable, safe building and working with the builder to ensure the building is completed on schedule and budget.

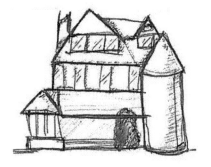

ARCHITECTURE RELATED CAREERS

So you now understand what Architects do, but what if you realize you don't want to be an Architect after all, and you still like the idea of working the field? There are still many other oc-cupations out there that have their hand in architecture without being an Architect. Making buildings is a team effort and there are many players in the industry, such as:

Civil Engineers
Structural Engineers
Mechanical, Electrical and Plumbing Engineers
Interior Designers
Landscape Architects
Lighting Designers
Roofing Consultants
Acoustic Consultants
Energy Consultants
Sustainability Consultants
Accessibility Consultants
General Contractors
Construction Managers
Specialty Contractors

ENGINEERS

While an Architect is responsible for the design of the building, there are many more things that need go into it to make the building work properly. Engineers are specialists that design very specific components of the building. They typically work under and are hired by the Architect to design these systems.

CIVIL ENGINEER
Civil Engineers are responsible for the area around the building and the components that tie into it. They work on items such as the grading of the lot (leveling for a building to sit on the ground), parking lots, and where utilities such as water, waste water and electricity come from and how they interact with the building design. Civil Engineers can also design items not related to buildings such as roads.

STRUCTURAL ENGINEER
Structural Engineers work hand in hand with the Architect to ensure that the building is capable of withstanding any loads placed upon it. Through calculation and modeling they will determine the best type of building structure and where to place items such as columns or beams. They will factor in such items as the weight of the building, the weight of the people and equipment in the building, wind loads, and seismic loads in order to ensure the building is safe.

M.E.P. ENGINEER
Mechanical, Electrical and Plumbing (MEP) Engineers deal with the components in a building that work behind the scenes. They design the heating, ventilation and air conditioning (HVAC) systems and ductwork, the electrical outlets and panels, and the plumbing lines. These engineers can be specialists in their given focus, or can engineer all three.

OTHER DESIGNERS

Architects are responsible for the overall design while engineers detail specific components, but there are other designers that can have a say in the look and feel of the building. These designers are specialists in a specific field related to the building and primarily focus on that portion.

INTERIOR DESIGN
Interior Designers are instrumental in designing a comfortable and functional space within the building. Sometimes Architects will fill this role, but there are times when one may need to rely on an Interior Designer's expertise in components such as color selection, finish selections and furniture selection. Interior Designers are typically also a licensed profession regulated by the State, but there are also those who work as Interior Decorators and they do finish and color selections with less regulation for the function and code related issues, as they are not licensed to be responsible for it.

LANDSCAPE ARCHITECTURE
Landscape Architects work in conjunction with the Architect and Civil Engineers to provide design aspects of the site. Their services typically include plant selections, irrigation details and site furnishings. They are typically a licensed profession as well and generally require education and examination as well.

LIGHTING DESIGN
Lighting Designers work with both Architects and Interior Designers when their expertise is needed. A lot of Architects and Interior Designers perform this role themselves, but there are many times when you would need a lighting designer's assistance in resolving issues with light levels, color temperature and fixture selection within the designed space.

SPECIALTY CONSULTANTS

Many consultants are similar to the other designers category, but they typically do not have a hand in the design or look and feel of the building or space. These consultants tend to straddle the line between designers and engineers and are influential in their given focus.

ROOFING CONSULTANTS
Roofing consultants focus on detailing the roof and all of its systems in order to ensure a weather-tight envelope. They tend to be experts in the many different roof types out there and how to apply each type to the specific design.

ACOUSTIC CONSULTANTS
Acoustic consultants may be brought in and utilized to enhance the sound properties of the space for specific needs. Through calculations and modeling they are able to produce dramatic changes in the room through orientation, layout and finishes. They are typically used in specific projects such as auditoriums, concert halls and even libraries in order to achieve a certain level of sound.

ENERGY CONSULTANTS
Energy Consultants are a specialized consultant that can focus on reducing the energy consumption of a building by modeling and calculations. They focus on the envelope, or skin, of the building, the insulation and systems in order to provide an efficient package. This role can sometime be filled by the MEP engineers as well.

SUSTAINABILITY CONSULTANTS

Sustainability Consultants will similarly focus on energy as well, but also look at everything from water usage to material selections. With the increased desire for LEED rated projects the need for sustainability consultants has increased. Sustainability consultants can advise on methods to achieve a LEED rating.

ACCESSIBILITY CONSULTANTS

Accessibility Consultants focus on specific aspects related to the design of a building so that it is usable for all people regardless of their abilities. They will advise on items such as wheelchair accessibility and accessibility for the vision or hearing impaired. They will advise on complying with applicable Acts such as the American with Disabilities Act (ADA).

CONSTRUCTION

Beyond the design of the building, there are infinitely more roles related to the construction of the building. Generally once the design is complete, it is handed over to somebody to build, and this is where contractors come into play.

GENERAL CONTRACTORS

General Contractors are the most common type of construction related career. General Contractors are responsible for taking the drawings from the Architect and Engineers and building it or organizing the trades who will be specializing in each aspect of building. They are responsible for the overall schedule and budget of the project and report directly to the owner. Many times the General Contractor will perform a lot of the construction tasks themselves.

CONSTRUCTION MANAGERS

Construction Managers are similar to general contractors except they do not always perform the construction tasks themselves. They can take the form of a Construction Manager at Risk, meaning they are responsible for organizing the sub-contractors, or Construction Manager as Agent, meaning they act as advisor to the owner only.

SPECIALTY CONTRACTORS

Subcontractors typically work under the General Contractor or Construction Manager and specialize in a specific trade such as plumbing, electrical, framing, drywall, painting, etc. They typically do not have contact with the owner or Architect, but will work through the general contractor or construction manager to produce the desired product.

CHAPTER 1: ACTION ITEM

1. Describe one building you visited today.

2. Who else might have been involved in the design of it?

3. How would you design it differently?

CHAPTER 2
ARCHITECTURE AS A CAREER

ARCHITECTURE POSITIONS/ROLES

So you still want to be an Architect? Great! But wait; there are still many different roles within an architecture firm and you should know them as well. These roles depend on the type of architecture firm and the project types/sizes they work on, but are generally listed below.

INTERN/DESIGNER
When you first start working at an architecture firm, you will typically fit into the Intern/Designer job description. Intern can mean so many different things in different industries, but in most it is meant as a student who works, sometimes for free, in order to get work experience in college. This is not what it means in Architecture. Nearly all States do not allow anybody to call themselves an Architect unless they are officially licensed, so this means most people, until they are licensed, are considered Architectural Interns. This can be somebody who is just starting out, to somebody who has been in the industry for year, but isn't licensed yet. Most importantly, in Architecture, it does not mean you are working for free.

DRAFTER/CAD TECHNICIAN/BIM TECHNICIAN
This role can sometimes be filled by interns, but is specifically focused on the production of the drawings needed to construct the building. Drafters are not typically responsible for design, construction observation or client interaction and are focused solely on the creation of drawings. They are experts in the use of computer programs and are responsible for the maintenance of the system and standards. Many times drafters can move up to become Job Captains who manage production departments or even Project Managers.

PROJECT ARCHITECT

Project Architects are usually used in larger firms who work on multiple projects. Their primary responsibility is to act as the Architect for that particular project. The may oversee the design, consultant coordination, client interaction and construction observation for the project. A project architect can be a senior employee, or can also be a junior employee who is capable of running a project independently.

PROJECT MANAGER

Similar to Project Architects, Project Managers work on a select number of projects in a larger firm. This role is usually used in firms where there may just be one head Architect who deals with the big-picture tasks, while the Project Managers deal with the day-to-day tasks. They may or may not be involved in the design, or client interactions, but they will generally deal with production, internal budget and schedules and consultant coordination.

ARCHITECT/PARTNER/PRINCIPAL

Depending on the firm, the head decision maker might just be called the Architect, or Partner/Principal. In small sole-practice firms, the Architect can be the owner, project manager, drafter and marketing director at the same time, but will generally just be referred to as the Architect. In larger firms with multiple Architects, the title of Partner or Principal signifies that they hold a leadership position in the firm and are generally responsible for big-picture tasks and don't always get involved in day-to-day activities.

ARCHITECTS SALARY

Unlike many careers where there is a set pay range for your level of experience and title, Architects work in many different areas, ranging in project types and firm sizes, and thus the amount of money Architects make varies wildly. Thankfully there are different resources we can use to get a gauge on what to expect and how much Architects make.

MORE THAN MONEY
Before we get into the facts and figures of an Architect's salary, we have to first ask the question, "Why does it matter?" I have done many career day's with high school students, and salary is almost always the first question that is asked. The usual response is that it doesn't matter what you make as long as you are happy, which for the most part is true, but I feel that it does still matter. It matters because you don't want to be so idealistic that you get taken advantage of, and you definitely don't want to starve. We have become so afraid to talk about money in our profession that it has almost become a dirty word. Of course you want make money, but that comes as a side-benefit to being able to do the work you love. I heard this quote recently from Walt Disney and I think it totally applies to architecture as well, "We don't make movies to make more money, we make money to make more movies." Stop right now. Re-read that. It's important to the discussion. What we do as Architects is not so we become rich, but rather to allow us to do it more.

BUREAU OF LABOR STATISTICS
The first place to visit for facts on an Architect's salary is the Bureau of Labor Statistics administered by the US Department of Labor as they have data on the "Occupational Outlook". According to their website, the 2010 Median Pay is $72,550 per year, or $34.88 per hour. Delving a little further, they state that the lowest 10% earned less than $42,860, while the highest

10% earned more than $119,000. That's a pretty big range there, so where would you fall into the picture? Unfortunately for these purposes, it depends on a multitude of factors. What size firm do you work at? What type of projects do you do? Where in the country are you? These are all factors that make up the wide variance.

COMPARISON
For comparison purposes, let's look at a few other occupations. Unlike Architects, Engineers are broken down by BLS based on the type of engineering they do. Civil Engineers have a median pay of $77,560, while Mechanical Engineers are nearly the same at $78,160. Now let's look at some other professional, non-architecture occupations. Lawyers median pay is $112,760, Dentists are at $146,920, and Physicians come in at $166,400. As you can see by these comparisons, Architects are on par with peers in the industry (Engineers), but well below "other professionals" outside of architecture. So if money is critically important to you, maybe you should look into those other occupations.

Bear in mind however, that these numbers are for professionally licensed individuals, so they mean to say that Licensed Architects and Professional Engineers, and actual Doctors make that amount of money, and doesn't take into account what level you are at before you become licensed. When you first get out of college, I guarantee you will not be making $72,550 as an Architectural Intern. Depending on the level of responsibility you have, your pay varies greatly.

AIA COMPENSATION REPORT - 2013
With the variance in positions, firms, location, etc, it is time to start looking at the American Institute of Architects (AIA) Com-

pensation Report. This report was last published in 2013 and is based on a survey they sent out to 10,059 architecture firms and the 1,023 responses. What is spectacular about this list is when you look at the break down. According to the report, an Architect I, or newly licensed Architect, averages $59,700 in the country. If you take that same Architect and look at it by region, you will find that, for example, in the New England area, they may make $64,700 and in the Mountain region, make $51,700. Following the same Architect, you find that in a small firm of less than 5 employees, they would actually make $53,300 and in a large firm of 250 employees plus, $64,900. You can do the same exercise for all levels including Intern I, or zero years' experience, for you particular situation and find where you should be.

I want to close by reiterating that for most of us, we don't do architecture because we hope to become ridiculously wealthy, and if you get into the profession hoping for that, you might want to consider another path. I personally practice architecture because I love what I do and I know that I can make a difference in people's lives, while still getting paid comfortably to do it. We may not make as much as lawyers or doctors, but I wouldn't want to do their job anyways, because I am happy with my chosen profession. So with that being said, how much does an Architect make? Enough to be able to keep doing architecture.

.

CHAPTER 2: ACTION ITEM

1. Make a list of all the things you enjoy to do in your free time.

2. Compare that list to the different roles you can fill in an Architecture firm.

3. Is there a clear correlation to what you enjoy to do and what you can do at a firm?

CHAPTER 3
SKILLS NEEDED TO BE AN ARCHITECT

BASIC SKILLS

Following the basic description of what an Architect does, the biggest skill an Architect needs is the ability to design. But what does that mean? Designing buildings means taking the requirements of what the building will be used for such as building size, how spaces are organized, and general feel of the spaces, and putting it together into a package that is usable, functional, and most of all, aesthetically pleasing. So the skill an Architect should have is the ability to creatively problem-solve.

The occupation is based upon that idea of problem solving. The owner has a problem; they want to build something that will meet a specific need, and you are hired to solve that problem by designing the building. Throughout the process, that skill continues as you will now have the problem of figuring out how to actually build the design and then the problem of making sure the owner can afford the building, etc.

"Do I need to know how to draw to be an Architect?" Not necessarily. Architects don't need to be great artists to be successful. They don't need to be able to perfectly replicate the human form on paper, but they have to be able to express their ideas to people through drawings. That is why Architects don't need to know how to draw in the traditional sense, but they need to know how to sketch. Sketching is the act of putting your ideas down on paper so others can understand them. The great thing about sketches is that they don't have to be perfect, in fact they shouldn't be. A good sketch is one that somebody other than yourself can understand, and you can later spend your time (often with computers) making it perfect.

"Do I need to be good at math to be an Architect?" Again, not necessarily. It is important that Architects are capable of doing simple math to locate parts of the building and calculate square footages, but they don't necessarily need to know how to calculate the loads on a column based on trigonometry and physics. These higher level math tasks are typically delegated to specially trained engineers who have training and experience in the area. The Architect only needs to understand the concepts to ensure their designs are possible before it gets to the engineers.

In order to become an Architect you need to have the ability to creatively problem solve, have the ability to sketch and have a passing knowledge of math, but that is just the tip of the iceberg. A successful Architect should also be knowledgeable about public speaking, politics, business, real estate, marketing, construction and environment, just to name a few. The biggest skill an Architect can have is the willingness and ability to learn many different things and apply them to their profession.

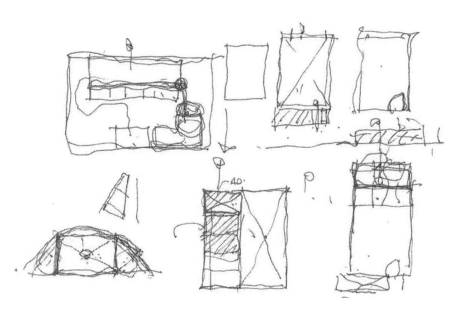

ADVANCED SKILLS

Beyond the mental ability to creatively problem solve and the ability to sketch, there are other skills that should be learned through school or work that can help you become a successful Architect.

HAND DRAFTING
With computer technology most Architects don't rely on hand drafting to produce construction documents anymore, but there is still value in knowing how to do it. By learning to hand draft, you learn the "art" of technical drawings. It is one thing to know how to control a computer to make lines on paper, but it is another thing entirely to know what those lines represent. Hand drafting forces you to slow down and contemplate what you are drawing. It forces you to understand line-weights and how they relate to what is being shown. It is crucial that the drawings you provide to a contractor are readable and make sense, and this is a skill you learn by hand drafting.

COMPUTER DRAFTING/MODELING
Once you understand why you need clear drawings, it is now a matter of knowing how to do that efficiently, and that is where computer drafting and modeling come into play. There are many programs out there, but currently the most common one is Autodesk AutoCAD for two-dimensional drafting and Autodesk Revit for three-dimensional building information modeling. These tools are essential to learn in order to produce good documents, but they can take a long time to learn. Another program that is used frequently in designing is Google's Sketchup. This program is free and relatively easy to learn, so it might be the best place to start for somebody just beginning in architecture.

PHYSICAL MODEL BUILDING

Throughout school and maybe even in work, you will be making a lot of physical models. These models can range from simple "study models" built out of cardboard or foam core, to final "presentation models" built out of basswood or other materials. The reason for these models is to be able to visualize a design in three-dimensions to get a better feel for the spaces.

CHAPTER 3: ACTION ITEM

1. Name three buildings you admire in your city

2. Visit one of the buildings and sit down for a few hours sketching out specific details

3. Build a model of it out of cardboard.

CHAPTER 4
ARCHITECTURE EDUCATION

UNIVERSITY ARCHITECTURE DEGREES

Your first step to becoming an Architect is to get your education. There are many ways you can get your education, depending on the State you are in, but in general most States require an accredited degree. Accredited degrees take a few forms, but the most important thing to remember is that it must be accredited by the National Architectural Accrediting Board, or NAAB. The two most common accredited degrees are the Bachelor of Architecture, B.Arch or the Master of Architecture, M.Arch. NAAB also accredits a Doctor of Architecture, D.Arch, but considering that there is only one university offering that degree, it is not very common. Currently NAAB lists 58 B.Arch programs and 95 M.Arch programs in the United States. For those in Canada, the accrediting board is the Canadian Architectural Certification Board, or CACB.

ACCREDITATION
NAAB is the only board with the authority to accredit architecture education in terms of providing B.Arch or M.Arch degrees. Their purpose is to have an independent third party review the quality of the education being provided and ensure that they are meeting the minimum requirements. This is done through cyclical audits where non-profit groups visit the campus and review student work that ranges from below-average, average, and above-average. This audit occurs on a cycle anywhere from two to six years. For a brand new program, they will typically have an "initial accreditation" that will last three years. After the initial accreditation the board will make a recommendation based on any deficiencies in the program. If the program is found to have severe enough deficiencies, they will be put on a two-year probation, and if they do not make corrections, their accreditation will be revoked. For major deficiencies not severe enough for probation, the school will re-

ceive a three-year accreditation, and for minor deficiencies an eight-year accreditation.

B. ARCH VS M. ARCH

Accredited schools offer a B.Arch, M.Arch or both. The B.Arch degree is a five-year professional degree that is generally considered equivalent to the M.Arch. The M.Arch degree is offered for those that already have a Bachelor's degree in another major (or in an non-accredited architecture degree). Some schools also offer what is referred to as an M.Arch 2, or post-professional degree for those with a B.Arch who chose to get an M.Arch as well. The M.Arch path is often referred to as a 4+2 program since you would typically have a four-year bachelor degree and you add on a two-year M.Arch degree.

WHICH IS BETTER?

Which degree you decide to go for will be determined by many conditions, with no one choice being better than the other. Some believe that a B.Arch degree is more beneficial because you get five years of architecture education, while others feel that having a degree in something else before coming to architecture will make you well rounded, and both of them are probably true in a lot of cases. Another reason to choose one over the other could be determined by your school of choice. Maybe your in-state school you really want to go to doesn't offer an accredited B.Arch or M.Arch degree. Your decision could also be determined by your timeline, whether you want a 5-year or 6-year program.

SCHOOLS

A list of accredited schools sorted by State can be found at the end of this book.

SELECTING A UNIVERSITY

Do a quick Internet search on the best architecture schools and you will find many differing opinions and ideas on what makes the best institution. There are so many different kinds of universities and each person is different, so it is impossible to say one is better than the other. There are a lot of generalities, and below is based on my experience with some schools, but this does not necessarily match everyone's experience, so you should really form an opinion for yourself.

ACCREDITED DEGREES
We talked about the importance of accredited degrees and that should be your first requirement in selecting a school. There are certainly other schools out there that have architecture related programs, but unless they are accredited by the National Architectural Accrediting Board, NAAB, they may not count towards your education requirement in your state. This first requirement will narrow down the list of architecture programs significantly and is not based on one person's opinion, but on a pre-determined set of requirements that identify the ability of the school to provide the required education.

PUBLIC VS. PRIVATE
Once you have narrowed down your search by accreditation, the next step is to choose between the other two types of schools, public vs private. State schools are state-funded institutions that offer education at a discounted rate for in-state students. If you are an out-of-state student, the tuition for these public schools can be a bit higher. Private schools primarily will receive their funding through tuition, endowments and other sources, thus typically having higher costs. The decision between these two types of institutions typically comes down to cost vs. education. In architecture however, going to a public institution does not mean receiving a "lesser" education. In fact

a lot of state schools rank higher in many polls over private institutions. I personally have gone to both types, a state school for undergraduate and private school for graduate, and I cannot say that either one was sub-par or superior to the other, but the costs were definitely different. Your choice will come down to where you want to go (in-state or out-of-state), if you can get any scholarships and how much you are expecting to spend on your education.

DESIGN PHILOSOPHY
Beyond the cost issues with public versus private institutions is the philosophy of each campus. Each university will have a particular focus and mission statement of what they are interested in teaching. Generally these schools fall into two categories, design schools vs. technical schools.

Design schools are those that focus on more theoretical ideas on what architecture is and tend to focus heavily on the design aspect of architecture. An example of this type of university, in my opinion, is SciARC in Los Angeles. I have been to many critiques (crits) at this school and the work showcases examples of some very extravagant designs that may or may not be build able, but the ideas behind them were strong.

Unlike design schools, technical schools tend to focus more on the reality of architecture and making architecture that is build able. An example I can think of for this type of school is of California Polytechnic University where they teach many practical skills in architecture in addition to design.

There are pros and cons to each, and a million different opinions on them. Some feel that design oriented schools allow for free-thinking and produce high design ability that will help once the student learns the real-world techniques though their work experience and they can combine the two. Others feel that the technical schools produce students that are better prepared to contribute as an Architect and get their designs built. There are also many schools that may fall in between these two categories as well, so the best way to decide on which is a better fit for you is to first visit their website and see if the work they are producing is something that speaks to you. Then you should visit the campuses you are interested in and see if you can sit in on a crit or studio session to get a real feel for what the culture is like and the type of work they are producing.

OTHER CRITERIA
There are other criteria which may be equally as important in selecting an architecture school such as the campus, studio atmosphere, the schools image and the alumni network. The campus is important because you will be spending a lot of time there and whether you are interested in having the full college experience or find it perfectly acceptable to go to a "commuter campus", a school where most people don't live on campus. The studio atmosphere is important for the same reason, you will spend a lot of time there, so make sure it is a place that you will enjoy being in. The schools image may help later in terms of how people view the education you received, and the alumni network is important when trying to find work and being able to give back.

OTHER PEOPLE'S OPINIONS
There are many criteria that you must personally decide upon to be able to say which school is best for you, but if you are like a lot of people you want to see other opinions, and that is where the rankings come in. The criteria publications use to decide which school is "best" differs, so you will have to keep

that in mind when looking at the rankings. The most commonly cited publication that ranks architecture schools is Design Intelligence and you can see for yourself how they rank the schools if you do a quick Internet search for them.

As you can see, the reasons for choosing one school over the other differ greatly and can only be decided by you. Whether you are looking for a private, design-oriented, high-image school, or a technical state school that will get you a good job, there are many options out there and there is certain to be one school that will be a great fit for you. If you are interested in learning more about the schools, visit their website or campuses and make an informed decision.

NON-ARCHITECTURE EDUCATION

When you are in architecture school, there is a set of required classes that you must take. You will probably have many years of design studio, you will need history, structures and maybe environmental design. You will be required to take math to a certain level and maybe physics as well, but if you truly want to be a great Architect, I would recommend you look beyond the required classes and take these electives as well. These electives have helped make me who I am as an Architect more than a lot of required courses.

ART/DRAWING
Taking an art class can be nerve wracking if you don't consider yourself an artist, or it can be a piece of cake if you are, but either way, enroll in a drawing class for the level you are at. There are many things you will learn about techniques of drawing, but the two biggest take away's from a drawing class is first, the confidence you will have when you finish and second the ability to slow down and really see what you are looking at. We see things all the time, but it isn't until we try to put it down on paper that we can really see it for what it is. It allows us to take time and see objects or spaces in relation to each other, in relation to light and relation to you, the viewer.

SPEECH
An absolute must for any aspiring architect is speech class. The number one fear, above death, height, spiders, etc, is public speaking, and as an Architect, you will be doing a lot of it, so you better get comfortable with it now. Speech class will teach you tips and tricks to get comfortable speaking in front of others like not using a crutch (cue cards, lectern), and flexing your muscles to loosen the tension, but most importantly it will force you to do it, and that is the only way to get comfortable with public speaking. After doing it a few times you will realize that it is not so bad.

BUSINESS AND/OR ACCOUNTING

As an Architect you will spend time designing buildings, but as a sole practitioner or principal, you will spend more time running a business. In the end, architecture is a business and if you want to be successful at it, you will need to treat it as such. Learn about simple bookkeeping, how to manage bank accounts and business communication in these business classes to set you up for success.

GRAPHIC DESIGN

Architects are visual people and as such, we need to be able to show our ideas in a graphic manner. You may have the greatest idea in the world, but unless you can express that to someone visually, it means nothing. When you are in school you will be able to speak about your projects, but often times in your career or in competitions, you will not be present to explain it, so the graphics have to speak for themselves on the boards. Remember, "boards win awards", and in order to have good boards, you need good graphic design.

OUTSIDE EDUCATION

Beyond your education in a University, there are other types of education you can gain. If you want to learn more about computer drafting or construction management that is not taught at a University, you could look into enrolling in a few classes at a trade school or local community college. You can also find a lot of information online if you are interested in learning more about graphics programs, drawing or drafting techniques.

APPLYING TO
ARCHITECTURE SCHOOL

Getting into architecture school can be incredibly difficult. Unlike many other majors out there, the number of applications versus the number of spots available in an architecture program is incredibly high. This is because there are only a limited number of accredited universities in the nation and they only take applications once a year.

WHEN TO START?
You want to get started on your application as soon as possible. Whether you are in high school, junior college or another career, the time to start thinking about your application is now. Nearly all universities accept applications for the Fall semester only, so that everyone goes through the system together and they all need to start at the same time.

HOW TO START?
The first thing you need to do is to identify the universities that you are interested in. Everyone will have their own criteria, but make sure it is a program you will be happy with and that it will match your goals. Once you have the schools identified, it's time to start doing some research. Find out what their application process is like and what you need to send in. Most likely the application packet will include items such as the application, a portfolio, transcripts from previous schools and test scores. Some will also require an essay and perhaps even an interview.

BEFORE THE APPLICATION
Before you start filling in the application and making your portfolio, you should also look into what other classes or extracurricular activities you should take to give you a better chance. If you have the time, look into taking extra classes at your local

community college or high school that will round out your skills and make you a better overall applicant. Also make sure you have met all of the universities requirements for prerequisite classes. Think about volunteering at local non-profit construction sites to show you have hands-on knowledge.

THE PORTFOLIO
The single most important portion of the application is the portfolio. This will hold true through the rest of your career as an Architect, so get used to it now. Your GPA, test scores and letters of recommendation are all important, but so long as you meet the minimums, and most applicants will, the portfolio will be what sets you apart.

What needs to go into the portfolio will vary depending on the school you are applying to and your experience. Each portfolio should be tailored to fit the university you are applying to. If you have identified a set of schools that are all heavy on digital fabrication and 3D-models, show that you are interested in that. If you are applying to a university focused on sustainability, show that you care about the same topic. What schools are looking for in candidates are people who will be a good fit for the program and can contribute back to the school.

If you have experience with architecture, feel free to include some samples, but remember that it is more important to show your process than your product. Don't just include a final rendering of the project, but also show the sketches you made in your thought process to get to that final design. Universities review portfolios to accept people into their program, not projects.

If you don't have any architecture experience, don't stress over that too much. If you already knew how to be an Architect, what would they have left to teach you? What you want to show is that you are capable of being an Architect. They want to see that you have an eye for design, whether it is architecture or not. Include photography, drawings, painting, furniture design, graphic design or product design. They want to see that you are capable of creative problem solving, which is the most important skill for an Architect to have.

CHAPTER 4: ACTION ITEM

1. Make a plan of your education goals.

2. What are your top 3 accredited architecture schools?

3. What classes will you take when you are there (or before you get there?)

CHAPTER 5
LICENSING

HOW TO GET YOUR LICENSE

The reason for licensing Architects is that it ensures the person practicing architecture has the abilities required to protect the "Health, Safety, and Welfare" of the public. If there were no licensing requirements and buildings the public used were designed by somebody without the proper training, it creates a huge risk for everyone and could cause major problems for society as a whole.

In order to go through the licensing process, you have to determine which state you want to practice in, as they all have slightly differing requirements.

Regardless of the state, there is a typical method to getting licensed, which is the go through "education, experience, and examination." This means that you must get the education you need through an accredited university, get the experience you need in the right areas and pass the exams that determine you have the minimum requirements necessary to protect the health, safety and welfare of the public.

There are various agencies that determine the requirements and help you get through the process for each phase. Each state will have their own licensing board who has the final say on whether you are allowed to practice architecture in that state. Nationally, there is an association of these state boards called the National Council of Registration Boards, or NCARB for short. The role of NCARB has increased throughout the years and many states are using them as a standard. NCARB is generally responsible for tracking and verifying your education and experience and administering the exams.

Once you have your education complete through a NAAB accredited university, you will need to continue learning through work hours. You are required to have a certain number of years or hours of experience, varying by state, in addition to your education before they allow you to take the exams. A lot of States currently do this through NCARB in their Intern Development Program, or IDP. The IDP is intended to make sure that you are not just working for a few years in the architecture field doing the same task, but actually learning what you need in all tasks in order to perform as an Architect. This program identifies areas that are required and how many hours you should have in each category before you can be licensed.

IDP 2.0 Categories:

Category 1: Predesign (260 hours)
1A. Programming (80 hours)
1B. Site and Building Analysis (80 hours)
1C. Project Cost and Feasibility (40 hours)
1D. Planning and Zoning Regulations (60 hours)

Category 2: Design (2,600 hours)
2A. Schematic Design (320 hours)
2B. Engineering Systems (360 hours)
2C. Construction Costs (120 hours)
2D. Codes and Regulations (120 hours)
2E. Design Development (320 hours)
2F. Construction Documents (1,200 hours)
2G. Material Selection and Specification (160 hours)

Category 3: Project Management (720 hours)
3A. Bidding and Contract Negotiation (120 hours)
3B. Construction Administration (240 hours)
3C. Construction Phase: Observation (120 hours)
3D. General Project Management (240 hours)

Category 4: Practice Management (160 hours)
4A. Business Operations (80 hours)
4B. Leadership and Service (80 hours)

Once you have your education and experience complete, you can now take your Architect Registration Exams, or ARE's. The ARE's are exams in different categories intended to ensure you have the minimum required ability to protect the health, safety and welfare of the public. These are exams that can be taken in any order at any time of the year, but you are required to pass all seven, and if you fail any of them, you need to retake them until you pass, in order to become licensed.

ARE 4.0 Sections

Programming, Planning and Practice
Site Planning & Design
Building Design & Construction Systems
Schematic Design
Structural Systems
Building Systems
Construction Documents and Services

The process described above is what has been setup by most states and NCARB as the typical path, but every state has different requirements, so see the end of this book for your specific State requirements.

CHAPTER 6
LICENSING WITHOUT A DEGREE

HOW TO GET YOUR LICENSE WITHOUT A UNIVERSITY DEGREE

In order to become a licensed Architect most states require you to have "Education, Experience, and Examination", but what if it isn't possible to get the education portion? Maybe you have to maintain a full-time job, maybe you can't afford it, or maybe there are no accredited schools near where you live. Whatever the reason, there are other ways to practice architecture without a college degree. Before we get to that though, let me be very clear here, architecture school is extremely valuable in the things you will learn and the connections you will make, and whatever reasons you have for not being able to go should really be re-considered. I was able to complete two degrees, get licensed, work a full-time job and another part-time job and raise a family all at the same time in 6 years. So believe me, it's not easy, but it is completely possible.

So you've still decided that it is not possible for you to get a degree in architecture, but you still want to work in architecture, that's fine, there are many ways to do it. The first option is to just not get licensed at all. Many states do not require an Architect's stamp for certain types of buildings. Many people who design these structures are referred to as Building Designers, and are capable of designing certain types of buildings. Keep in mind though, that without the license, you are not held responsible for protecting the health, safety and welfare of the public and you should choose your projects wisely. There are many examples of people who also practice design of large buildings without a license, but they have an Architect working with them to review the drawings. Whatever you do, do not ask an Architect to just stamp the plans for you, as it is illegal for an Architect to "plan stamp" without having reasonable control or review of the drawings that were produced. Another important note, if you decide to go this route, do not call yourself an

Architect or anything similar to that term, as that is reserved for licensed professionals only and you could get fined.

Maybe being a Building Designer isn't for you and you want to be a grade-A certified licensed Architect. Well you still can, even without a degree, but it will be a little more difficult. There are still a few states that allow you to substitute work experience for a degree, and this will be your way in. The states that do not require an accredited degree are:

- Arizona
- California
- Colorado
- Hawaii
- Idaho
- Illinois
- Maine
- Maryland
- New Hampshire
- New York
- Oklahoma
- Tennessee
- Vermont
- Washington
- Wisconsin

So if you happen to live in, and want to practice in, one of those states, congratulations, you don't need an accredited degree to become licensed! You will still have to put in more years of experience and still pass the tests just like everyone else though. If you don't live in any of those states listed, don't fret, there is another workaround. Of all of those states, only Tennessee requires you to be a resident of that state to get a license there. So here's what you do, start your Internship Development Program (IDP) with NCARB immediately, when you are ready to start taking your tests, do it through one of those states. The tests are administered through computer and can be taken anywhere, so you can still test in your home state. Keep in mind however that states like California and Oklahoma also have a state specific test that you will have to pass as well, most likely administered in that state. Once you pass the test, congratulations again, you are licensed to practice architecture...in that state only. You now need to get reciprocity in your home state.

There are two ways to get reciprocity in your home state, the first requires you to contact your accrediting board and send them the information from the state you were licensed in, the other way is to get an NCARB Certificate. Which you choose depends on your comfort level with getting all the information you need from the state or if you are willing to pay NCARB to do it for you. If you go the NCARB Certificate route, it makes it extremely easy to do, but will cost you to initiate and receive the certificate, as well as money every year to renew and keep active. If you want to stop renewing it after you get your license, you certainly can, but if you ever want to get a license in any other states, it will cost even more money to start the certification process over again. I personally decided to go the NCARB certificate route when I switched states because it was much easier and let me put five more letters after my name.

CHAPTER 7
CONCLUSION

NEXT STEPS

Architecture is an amazing career that can offer you enjoyment through job freedom and making a difference in people's lives. You will be able to design structures that directly impact people and are felt every day while offering you an artistic outlet mixed with equal parts science, math and business. Architecture is so varied, anybody with a passing interest in it can find a good fit for their abilities and they can be successful in a lot of fields. It is not easy to become an Architect and there is a lot to learn, but in the end it is worth it to have a fulfilling occupation that is well respected and enjoyable.

If after reading this you feel that architecture might be a good fit for you, take the next step and sign up for some architecture classes at your local community college, stop in and talk to a local Architect, or just enroll in the University of your choice.

THANK YOU!

Thank you for taking the time to read this guide. I hope you enjoyed it and find it useful. I appreciate the continued support and thank you for taking the time to read through it.
Please leave a comment on the www.architecturecareerguide. com website or send me an email if you have questions or a success story to tell. I look forward to hearing how you have reached your goals.

APPENDIX A: RESOURCES

Here are some books that I have found helpful and are full of great information:

Architecture: Form, Space and Order, Francis D. K. Ching, ISBN: 0471752169

Building Construction Illustrated, Francis D. K. Ching, ISBN: 0470087811

A History of Architecture: Settings and Rituals, Spiro Kostof, ISBN: 9780195083798

101 Things I Learned in Architecture School, Matthew Frederick, ISBN: 0262062666

Design Like you Give a Damn, Stohr and Cameron Sinclair, ISBN: 1933045256

Precedents in Architecture, Roger H. Clark, ISBN: 0470946741

APPENDIX B: NAAB ACCREDITED UNIVERSITIES

ALABAMA

Auburn University - B. Arch.
Tuskegee University - B. Arch.

ARIZONA

Arizona State University - M. Arch.
University of Arizona - B. Arch.;
Frank Lloyd Wright School of Architecture - M. Arch.

ARKANSAS

University of Arkansas - B. Arch.

CALIFORNIA

Academy of Art University - M. Arch.
University of California at Berkeley - M. Arch.
University of California at Los Angeles - M. Arch.
California College of the Arts - B. Arch.; M. Arch.
California Polytechnic State University –
San Luis Obispo - B. Arch.
California State Polytechnic University -
Pomona - B. Arch.; M. Arch.
NewSchool of Architecture & Design -
B. Arch.; M. Arch.
Southern California Institute of Architecture
(SCI-ARC) - B. Arch.; M. Arch.
University of Southern California - B. Arch.; M. Arch.
Woodbury University - B. Arch.; M. Arch.

COLORADO

University of Colorado at Denver - M. Arch.

CONNECTICUT

University of Hartford - M. Arch.
Yale University - M. Arch.

DISTRICT OF COLUMBIA

The Catholic University of America - M. Arch.
Howard University - B. Arch.

FLORIDA

Florida A&M University - B. Arch.; M. Arch.
Florida Atlantic University - B. Arch.
Florida International University - M. Arch.
University of Florida - M. Arch.
University of Miami - B. Arch.; M. Arch.
University of South Florida - M. Arch.

GEORGIA

Georgia Institute of Technology - M. Arch.
Savannah College of Arts & Design - M. Arch.
Southern Polytechnic State University - B. Arch.

HAWAII

University of Hawaii at Manoa - D. Arch.

IDAHO

University of Idaho - M. Arch.

ILLINOIS

Illinois Institute of Technology - B. Arch.; M. Arch.
University of Illinois at Chicago - M. Arch.
University of Illinois at Urbana-Champaign - M. Arch.
Judson University - M. Arch.
The School of the Art Institute of Chicago - M. Arch.
Southern Illinois University Carbondale - M. Arch.

INDIANA

Ball State University - M. Arch.
University of Notre Dame - B. Arch.; M. Arch.

IOWA

Iowa State University - B. Arch.; M. Arch.

KANSAS

Kansas State University - M. Arch.
University of Kansas - M. Arch.

KENTUCKY

University of Kentucky - M. Arch.

LOUISIANA

University of Louisiana at Lafayette - M. Arch.
Louisiana State University – B. Arch.; M. Arch.
Louisiana Tech University - M. Arch.
Southern University and A&M College - B. Arch.
Tulane University - M. Arch.

MARYLAND

University of Maryland - M. Arch.
Morgan State University - M. Arch.

MASSACHUSETTS

Boston Architectural College - B. Arch.; M. Arch.
Harvard University - M. Arch.
University of Massachusetts Amherst - M. Arch.
Massachusetts Institute of Technology - M. Arch.
Northeastern University - M. Arch.
Wentworth Institute of Technology - M. Arch.

MICHIGAN

Andrews University - M. Arch.
University of Detroit Mercy - M. Arch.
Lawrence Technological University - M. Arch.
University of Michigan - M. Arch.

MINNESOTA

University of Minnesota - M. Arch.

MISSISSIPPI

Mississippi State University - B. Arch.

MISSOURI

Drury College Hammons - M. Arch.
Washington University in St. Louis - M. Arch.

MONTANA

Montana State University - M. Arch.

NEBRASKA

University of Nebraska-Lincoln - M. Arch.

NEVADA

University of Nevada - Las Vegas - M. Arch.

NEW JERSEY

New Jersey Institute of Technology - B. Arch.; M. Arch.
Princeton University - M. Arch.

NEW MEXICO

University of New Mexico - M. Arch.

NEW YORK

City College of The City University of New York -
B. Arch.; M. Arch.
Columbia University -M. Arch.
The Cooper Union - B. Arch.
Cornell University - B. Arch.; M. Arch.
New York Institute of Technology - B. Arch.
Parsons School of Design - M. Arch.
Pratt Institute - B. Arch.; M. Arch.
Rensselaer Polytechnic Institute - B. Arch.; M. Arch.
State University of New York at Buffalo - M. Arch.
Syracuse University - B. Arch.; M. Arch.

NORTH CAROLINA

University of North Carolina at Charlotte -
B. Arch.; M. Arch.
North Carolina State University - B. Arch.; M. Arch.

NORTH DAKOTA

North Dakota State University - M. Arch.

OHIO

University of Cincinnati - M. Arch.
Kent State University - M. Arch.
Miami University - M. Arch.
Ohio State University - M. Arch.

OKLAHOMA

Oklahoma State University - B. Arch.
University of Oklahoma - B. Arch.; M. Arch.

OREGON

University of Oregon - B. Arch.; M. Arch.
Portland State University - M. Arch.

PENNSYLVANIA

Carnegie Mellon University - B. Arch.
Drexel University - B. Arch.
Pennsylvania State University - B. Arch.
University of Pennsylvania - M. Arch.
Philadelphia University - B. Arch.
Temple University - B. Arch.; M. Arch.

RHODE ISLAND

Rhode Island School of Design - B. Arch.; M. Arch.
Roger Williams University - M. Arch.

SOUTH CAROLINA

Clemson University - M. Arch.

TENNESSEE

University of Memphis - M. Arch.
University of Tennessee-Knoxville - B. Arch.; M. Arch.

TEXAS

University of Houston - B. Arch.; M. Arch.
Prairie View A&M University - M. Arch.
Rice University - B. Arch.; M. Arch.
Texas A&M University - M. Arch.
University of Texas at Arlington - M. Arch.
University of Texas at Austin - B. Arch.; M. Arch.
University of Texas at San Antonio - M. Arch.
Texas Tech University - M. Arch.

UTAH

University of Utah - M. Arch.

VERMONT

Norwich University - M. Arch.

VIRGINIA

Hampton University - M. Arch.
Virginia Tech - B. Arch.; M. Arch.
University of Virginia - M. Arch.

WASHINGTON

University of Washington - M. Arch.
Washington State University - M. Arch.

WISCONSIN

University of Wisconsin-Milwaukee - M. Arch.

APPENDIX C: STATE LICENSING REQUIREMENTS

ALABAMA:

The licensing requirements for Alabama follow a more traditional approach of requiring a professional degree, completion of the Internship Development Program (IDP) and completion of the Architect Registration Exams (ARE).

Candidates can also begin taking the ARE's before they have completed the Internship Development Program, which helps to save some time.

How to become an Architect in Alabama:

1.Complete a professional degree (B.Arch, M.Arch, D.Arch) from a National Architectural Accrediting Board (NAAB) accredited University.

2.Completion of Intern Development Program (IDP) as administered by the National Council of Architectural Registration Boards (NCARB)

3. Successful completion of Architect Registration Exam (ARE) as administered by the National Council of Architectural Registration Boards (NCARB)

To find more information on licensing requirements visit http://www.boa.alabama.gov/

ALASKA:

The licensing requirements for Alaska follow a more traditional approach of requiring a professional degree, completion of the Internship Development Program (IDP) and completion of the Architect Registration Exams (ARE).

Candidates can also begin taking the ARE's before they have completed the Internship Development Program, which helps to save some time.

How to become an Architect in Alaska:

1. Complete a professional degree (B.Arch, M.Arch, D.Arch) from a National Architectural Accrediting Board (NAAB) accredited University.

2. Completion of Intern Development Program (IDP) as administered by the National Council of Architectural Registration Boards (NCARB)

3. Successful completion of Architect Registration Exam (ARE) as administered by the National Council of Architectural Registration Boards (NCARB)

To find more information on licensing requirements visit http://commerce.alaska.gov/dnn/cbpl/Home.aspx

ARIZONA:

The licensing requirements for Arizona allow for various degree paths, do not require completion of the Internship Development Program (IDP) and but do require completion of the Architect Registration Exams (ARE).

Candidates can also begin taking the ARE's before they have completed the Internship Development Program, which helps to save some time.

How to become an Architect in Arizone:

1. Complete a professional degree (B.Arch, M.Arch, D.Arch) from a National Architectural Accrediting Board (NAAB) accredited University, or a four-year degree plus 5 years professional experience, or 8 years professional experience only.

2. Completion of 96 months of professional experience

3. Successful completion of Architect Registration Exam (ARE) as administered by the National Council of Architectural Registration Boards (NCARB)

To find more information on licensing requirements visit http://www.azbtr.gov/

ARKANSAS:
The licensing requirements for Arkansas follow a more traditional approach of requiring a professional degree, completion of the Internship Development Program (IDP) and completion of the Architect Registration Exams (ARE).

Candidates can also begin taking the ARE's before they have completed the Internship Development Program, which helps to save some time.

How to become an Architect in Arkansas:

1. Complete a professional degree (B.Arch, M.Arch, D.Arch) from a National Architectural Accrediting Board (NAAB) accredited University.

2. Completion of Intern Development Program (IDP) as administered by the National Council of Architectural Registration Boards (NCARB)

3. Successful completion of Architect Registration Exam (ARE) as administered by the National Council of Architectural Registration Boards (NCARB)

To find more information on licensing requirements visit http://asbalaid.arkansas.gov/Pages/default.aspx

CALIFORNIA:

California is one of the more lenient states in terms of the type of education and experience needed in order to become licensed. Candidates can apply as soon as they have 8 years of experience which can be through school, work and/or combination of the two. Candidates are also required to complete the Internship Development Program (IDP), which ensures the proper type of experience is acquired, completion of the Architect Registration Exam (ARE) as well as an additional examination requirement beyond the Architectural Registration Exam, which test candidates on State specific issues.

How to become an Architect in California:

1. Complete 8 years of experience or the equivalent.

*8 years can be completed in numerous ways based on the Table of Equivalents:
5 years for NAAB accredited degree
4 years for non-NAAB accredited 5-year degree program
3.5 years for four-year architecture degree
2 years for degree which consists of a four-year curriculum in field related to Architecture
1 year for any other four-year degree
6 months for two-year degree (city/community college)
1 year for city/community college degree or technical school certificate in field related to architecture
Any number of years of work experience as indicated in Table of Equivalents

2. Completion of Intern Development Program (IDP) as administered by the National Council of Architectural Registration Boards (NCARB)

3. Successful completion of Architect Registration Exam (ARE) as administered by the National Council of Architectural Registration Boards (NCARB)

4. Success completion of the California Supplemental Exam

To find more information on licensing requirements visit http://www.cab.ca.gov/candidates/license_requirements.shtml

COLORADO:
The licensing requirements for Colorado allow for various degree paths, and will require completion of the Internship Development Program (IDP) in 2014 along with completion of the Architect Registration Exams (ARE).

Candidates can also begin taking the ARE's before they have completed the Internship Development Program, which helps to save some time.

How to become an Architect in Colorado:

1. Completion of a combination of degree and experience hours as follows:
- B.Arch + 3 years professional experience
- M.Arch + 3 years professional experience
- Four-year Architecture Degree + 5 years professional experience
- Four-year related Degree + 7 years professional experience
- Four-year BA or BS Degree + 8 years professional experience
- AA or AS in Architecture + 8 years professional experience
- AA or AS non-related Degree + 9 years professional experience
- No Degree + 10 years professional experience

3. Successful completion of Architect Registration Exam (ARE) as administered by the National Council of Architectural Registration Boards (NCARB)

To find more information on licensing requirements visit http://cdn.colorado.gov/cs/Satellite/DORA-Reg/CBON/DORA/1251632130538

CONNECTICUT:
The licensing requirements for Connecticut follow a more traditional approach of requiring a professional degree, completion of the Internship Development Program (IDP) and completion of the Architect Registration Exams (ARE).

How to become an Architect in Connecticut:

1. Complete a professional degree (B.Arch, M.Arch, D.Arch) from a National Architectural Accrediting Board (NAAB) accredited University.

2. Completion of Intern Development Program (IDP) as administered by the National Council of Architectural Registration Boards (NCARB)

3. Successful completion of Architect Registration Exam (ARE) as administered by the National Council of Architectural Registration Boards (NCARB)

To find more information on licensing requirements visit http://www.ct.gov/dcp/site/default.asp

DELAWARE:

The licensing requirements for Delaware follow a more traditional approach of requiring a professional degree, completion of the Internship Development Program (IDP) and completion of the Architect Registration Exams (ARE).

Candidates can also begin taking the ARE's before they have completed the Internship Development Program, which helps to save some time.

How to become an Architect in Delaware:

1. Complete a professional degree (B.Arch, M.Arch, D.Arch) from a National Architectural Accrediting Board (NAAB) accredited University.

2. Completion of Intern Development Program (IDP) as administered by the National Council of Architectural Registration Boards (NCARB)

3. Successful completion of Architect Registration Exam (ARE) as administered by the National Council of Architectural Registration Boards (NCARB)

To find more information on licensing requirements visit http://www.dpr.delaware.gov/boards/architects

DISTRICT OF COLUMBIA:
The licensing requirements for Washington DC follow a more traditional approach of requiring a professional degree, completion of the Internship Development Program (IDP) and completion of the Architect Registration Exams (ARE).

Candidates can also begin taking the ARE's before they have completed the Internship Development Program, which helps to save some time.

How to become an Architect in Washington DC:

1. Complete a professional degree (B.Arch, M.Arch, D.Arch) from a National Architectural Accrediting Board (NAAB) accredited University.

2. Completion of Intern Development Program (IDP) as administered by the National Council of Architectural Registration Boards (NCARB)

3. Successful completion of Architect Registration Exam (ARE) as administered by the National Council of Architectural Registration Boards (NCARB)

To find more information on licensing requirements visit http://www.vue.com/dc/arch_intdes/

FLORIDA:
The licensing requirements for Florida follow a more traditional approach of requiring a professional degree, completion of the Internship Development Program (IDP) and completion of the Architect Registration Exams (ARE).

Candidates can also begin taking the ARE's before they have completed the Internship Development Program, which helps to save some time.

How to become an Architect in Florida:

1. Complete a professional degree (B.Arch, M.Arch, D.Arch) from a National Architectural Accrediting Board (NAAB) accredited University.

2. Completion of Intern Development Program (IDP) as administered by the National Council of Architectural Registration Boards (NCARB)

3. Successful completion of Architect Registration Exam (ARE) as administered by the National Council of Architectural Registration Boards (NCARB)

To find more information on licensing requirements visit http://www.myfloridalicense.com/dbpr/pro/arch/index.html/

GEORGIA:
The licensing requirements for Georgia follow a more traditional approach of requiring a professional degree, completion of the Internship Development Program (IDP) and completion of the Architect Registration Exams (ARE).

Candidates can also begin taking the ARE's before they have completed the Internship Development Program, which helps to save some time

How to become an Architect in Georgia:

1. Complete a professional degree (B.Arch, M.Arch, D.Arch) from a National Architectural Accrediting Board (NAAB) accredited University.

2. Completion of Intern Development Program (IDP) as administered by the National Council of Architectural Registration Boards (NCARB)

3. Successful completion of Architect Registration Exam (ARE) as administered by the National Council of Architectural Registration Boards (NCARB)

To find more information on licensing requirements visit http://sos.georgia.gov/plb/architects

HAWAII:
The licensing requirements for Hawaii allow for various degree paths, completion of the Internship Development Program (IDP) if with a professional degree and completion of the Architect Registration Exams (ARE).

Candidates can also begin taking the ARE's before they have completed the Internship Development Program, which helps to save some time.

How to become an Architect in Hawaii:

1. Complete a professional degree (B.Arch, M.Arch, D.Arch) from a National Architectural Accrediting Board (NAAB) accredited University, or a four-year degree plus 5 years professional experience, or 11 years professional experience only.

2. Completion of Intern Development Program (IDP) as administered by the National Council of Architectural Registration Boards (NCARB) if combined with professional degree

3. Successful completion of Architect Registration Exam (ARE) as administered by the National Council of Architectural Registration Boards (NCARB)

To find more information on licensing requirements visit http://hawaii.gov/dcca/pvl/boards/engineer

IDAHO:

The licensing requirements for Idaho allows for various degree paths, completion of the Internship Development Program (IDP) and completion of the Architect Registration Exams (ARE).

Candidates can also begin taking the ARE's before they have completed the Internship Development Program, which helps to save some time.

How to become an Architect in Idaho:

1. Complete a professional degree (B.Arch, M.Arch, D.Arch) from a National Architectural Accrediting Board (NAAB) accredited University, or 8 years of professional experience only with completion of IDP.

2. Completion of Intern Development Program (IDP) as administered by the National Council of Architectural Registration Boards (NCARB)

3. Successful completion of Architect Registration Exam (ARE) as administered by the National Council of Architectural Registration Boards (NCARB)

To find more information on licensing requirements visit http:// ibol.idaho.gov/IBOL/Home.aspx

ILLINOIS:

The licensing requirements for Illinois allows for various degree paths (until 2014), completion of the Internship Development Program (IDP) and completion of the Architect Registration Exams (ARE), plus an additional state requirement.

Candidates can also begin taking the ARE's before they have completed the Internship Development Program, which helps to save some time.

How to become an Architect in Illinois:

1. Complete a professional degree (B.Arch, M.Arch, D.Arch) from a National Architectural Accrediting Board (NAAB) accredited University, or a four-year degree plus 5 years of professional experience and double of the required NCARB hours.

2. Completion of Intern Development Program (IDP) as administered by the National Council of Architectural Registration Boards (NCARB)

3. Successful completion of Architect Registration Exam (ARE) as administered by the National Council of Architectural Registration Boards (NCARB)

4. Completion of Affidavit showing you have read and understood the Illinois Architecture Practice Act & Administrative Rules

To find more information on licensing requirements visit http://www.idfpr.com/profs/info/architect.asp

INDIANA:
The licensing requirements for Indiana follow a more traditional approach of requiring a professional degree, completion of the Internship Development Program (IDP) and completion of the Architect Registration Exams (ARE).

Candidates can also begin taking the ARE's before they have completed the Internship Development Program, which helps to save some time.

How to become an Architect in Indiana:

1. Complete a professional degree (B.Arch, M.Arch, D.Arch) from a National Architectural Accrediting Board (NAAB) accredited University.

2. Completion of Intern Development Program (IDP) as administered by the National Council of Architectural Registration Boards (NCARB)

3. Successful completion of Architect Registration Exam (ARE) as administered by the National Council of Architectural Registration Boards (NCARB)

To find more information on licensing requirements visit http://www.in.gov/pla/architect.htm

IOWA:

The licensing requirements for Iowa follow a more traditional approach of requiring a professional degree, completion of the Internship Development Program (IDP) and completion of the Architect Registration Exams (ARE).

Candidates can also begin taking the ARE's before they have completed the Internship Development Program, which helps to save some time.

How to become an Architect in Iowa:

1. Complete a professional degree (B.Arch, M.Arch, D.Arch) from a National Architectural Accrediting Board (NAAB) accredited University.

2. Completion of Intern Development Program (IDP) as administered by the National Council of Architectural Registration Boards (NCARB)

3. Successful completion of Architect Registration Exam (ARE) as administered by the National Council of Architectural Registration Boards (NCARB)

To find more information on licensing requirements visit http://www.state.ia.us/government/com/prof/architect/home.html

KANSAS:

The licensing requirements for Kansas follow a more traditional approach of requiring a professional degree, completion of the Internship Development Program (IDP) and completion of the Architect Registration Exams (ARE).

Candidates can also begin taking the ARE's before they have completed the Internship Development Program, which helps to save some time.

How to become an Architect in Kansas:

1. Complete a professional degree (B.Arch, M.Arch, D.Arch) from a National Architectural Accrediting Board (NAAB) accredited University.

2. Completion of Intern Development Program (IDP) as administered by the National Council of Architectural Registration Boards (NCARB)

3. Successful completion of Architect Registration Exam (ARE) as administered by the National Council of Architectural Registration Boards (NCARB)

To find more information on licensing requirements visit http://www.ksbtp.ks.gov

KENTUCKY:

The licensing requirements for Kentucky follow a more traditional approach of requiring a professional degree, completion of the Internship Development Program (IDP) and completion of the Architect Registration Exams (ARE).

Candidates can also begin taking the ARE's before they have completed the Internship Development Program, which helps to save some time.

How to become an Architect in Kentucky:

1. Complete a professional degree (B.Arch, M.Arch, D.Arch) from a National Architectural Accrediting Board (NAAB) accredited University.

2. Completion of Intern Development Program (IDP) as administered by the National Council of Architectural Registration Boards (NCARB)

3. Successful completion of Architect Registration Exam (ARE) as administered by the National Council of Architectural Registration Boards (NCARB)

To find more information on licensing requirements visit http://boa.ky.gov/Pages/default.aspx

LOUISIANA:

The licensing requirements for Louisiana follow a more traditional approach of requiring a professional degree, completion of the Internship Development Program (IDP) and completion of the Architect Registration Exams (ARE).

Candidates can also begin taking the ARE's before they have completed the Internship Development Program, which helps to save some time.

How to become an Architect in Louisiana:

1. Complete a professional degree (B.Arch, M.Arch, D.Arch) from a National Architectural Accrediting Board (NAAB) accredited University.

2. Completion of Intern Development Program (IDP) as administered by the National Council of Architectural Registration Boards (NCARB)

3. Successful completion of Architect Registration Exam (ARE) as administered by the National Council of Architectural Registration Boards (NCARB)

To find more information on licensing requirements visit http://www.lastbdarchs.com

MAINE:
The licensing requirements for Maine allow for various degree paths, require completion of the Internship Development Program (IDP) and completion of the Architect Registration Exams (ARE).

How to become an Architect in Maine:

1. Complete a professional degree (B.Arch, M.Arch, D.Arch) from a National Architectural Accrediting Board (NAAB) accredited University, or a four-year degree plus 9 years of professional experience, or 13 years of professional experience only.

2. Completion of Intern Development Program (IDP) as administered by the National Council of Architectural Registration Boards (NCARB)

3. Successful completion of Architect Registration Exam (ARE) as administered by the National Council of Architectural Registration Boards (NCARB)

To find more information on licensing requirements visit http://www.maine.gov/pfr/professionallicensing/professions/architects

MARYLAND:

The licensing requirements for Maryland have education flexibility, but still require completion of the Internship Development Program (IDP) and completion of the Architect Registration Exams (ARE).

How to become an Architect in Maryland:

1. Completion of a professional degree, or a four-year degree plus 9 years of professional experience, or 13 years of only professional experience

2. Completion of Intern Development Program (IDP) as administered by the National Council of Architectural Registration Boards (NCARB)

3. Successful completion of Architect Registration Exam (ARE) as administered by the National Council of Architectural Registration Boards (NCARB)

To find more information on licensing requirements visit http://www.www.dllr.state.md.us/license/arch/

MASSACHUSETTS:

The licensing requirements for Massachusetts follow a more traditional approach of requiring a professional degree, completion of the Internship Development Program (IDP) and completion of the Architect Registration Exams (ARE).

Candidates can also begin taking the ARE's before they have completed the Internship Development Program, which helps to save some time.

How to become an Architect in Massachusetts:

1. Complete a professional degree (B.Arch, M.Arch, D.Arch) from a National Architectural Accrediting Board (NAAB) accredited University.

2. Completion of Intern Development Program (IDP) as administered by the National Council of Architectural Registration Boards (NCARB)

3. Successful completion of Architect Registration Exam (ARE) as administered by the National Council of Architectural Registration Boards (NCARB)

To find more information on licensing requirements visit http://www.mass.gov/ocabr/licensee/dpl-board/ar

MICHIGAN:

The licensing requirements for Michigan follow a more traditional approach of requiring a professional degree, completion of the Internship Development Program (IDP) and completion of the Architect Registration Exams (ARE).

Candidates can also begin taking the ARE's before they have completed the Internship Development Program, which helps to save some time.

How to become an Architect in Michigan:

1. Complete a professional degree (B.Arch, M.Arch, D.Arch) from a National Architectural Accrediting Board (NAAB) accredited University.

2. Completion of Intern Development Program (IDP) as administered by the National Council of Architectural Registration Boards (NCARB)

3. Successful completion of Architect Registration Exam (ARE) as administered by the National Council of Architectural Registration Boards (NCARB)

To find more information on licensing requirements visit http://www.michigan.gov/lara

MINNESOTA:
The licensing requirements for Minnesota follow a more traditional approach of requiring a professional degree, completion of the Internship Development Program (IDP) and completion of the Architect Registration Exams (ARE).

Candidates can also begin taking the ARE's before they have completed the Internship Development Program, which helps to save some time.

How to become an Architect in Minnesota:

1. Complete a professional degree (B.Arch, M.Arch, D.Arch) from a National Architectural Accrediting Board (NAAB) accredited University.

2. Completion of Intern Development Program (IDP) as administered by the National Council of Architectural Registration Boards (NCARB)

3. Successful completion of Architect Registration Exam (ARE) as administered by the National Council of Architectural Registration Boards (NCARB)

To find more information on licensing requirements visit http://mn.gov/aelslag

MISSISSIPPI:

The licensing requirements for Mississippi follow a more traditional approach of requiring a professional degree, completion of the Internship Development Program (IDP) and completion of the Architect Registration Exams (ARE), and completion of an additional exam.

Candidates can also begin taking the ARE's before they have completed the Internship Development Program, which helps to save some time.

How to become an Architect in Mississippi:

1. Complete a professional degree (B.Arch, M.Arch, D.Arch) from a National Architectural Accrediting Board (NAAB) accredited University.

2. Completion of Intern Development Program (IDP) as administered by the National Council of Architectural Registration Boards (NCARB)

3. Successful completion of Architect Registration Exam (ARE) as administered by the National Council of Architectural Registration Boards (NCARB)

4. Successful completion of State administered Jurisprudence Exam

To find more information on licensing requirements visit http://www.archbd.state.ms.us

MISSOURI:
The licensing requirements for Missouri follow a more traditional approach of requiring a professional degree, completion of the Internship Development Program (IDP) and completion of the Architect Registration Exams (ARE).

Candidates can also begin taking the ARE's before they have completed the Internship Development Program, which helps to save some time.

How to become an Architect in Missouri:

1. Complete a professional degree (B.Arch, M.Arch, D.Arch) from a National Architectural Accrediting Board (NAAB) accredited University.

2. Completion of Intern Development Program (IDP) as administered by the National Council of Architectural Registration Boards (NCARB)

3. Successful completion of Architect Registration Exam (ARE) as administered by the National Council of Architectural Registration Boards (NCARB)

To find more information on licensing requirements visit http://pr.mo.gov/apelsla.asp

MONTANA:

The licensing requirements for Montana follow a more traditional approach of requiring a professional degree, completion of the Internship Development Program (IDP) and completion of the Architect Registration Exams (ARE).

Candidates can also begin taking the ARE's before they have completed the Internship Development Program, which helps to save some time.

How to become an Architect in Montana:

1. Complete a professional degree (B.Arch, M.Arch, D.Arch) from a National Architectural Accrediting Board (NAAB) accredited University.

2. Completion of Intern Development Program (IDP) as administered by the National Council of Architectural Registration Boards (NCARB)

3. Successful completion of Architect Registration Exam (ARE) as administered by the National Council of Architectural Registration Boards (NCARB)

To find more information on licensing requirements visit http://bsd.dli.mt.gov/bsd_boards/arc_board/board_page.asp

NEBRASKA:

The licensing requirements for Nebraska follow a more traditional approach of requiring a professional degree, completion of the Internship Development Program (IDP) and completion of the Architect Registration Exams (ARE), but also require and additional state exam.

Candidates can also begin taking the ARE's before they have completed the Internship Development Program, which helps to save some time.

How to become an Architect in Nebraska:

1. Complete a professional degree (B.Arch, M.Arch, D.Arch) from a National Architectural Accrediting Board (NAAB) accredited University.

2. Completion of Intern Development Program (IDP) as administered by the National Council of Architectural Registration Boards (NCARB)

3. Successful completion of Architect Registration Exam (ARE) as administered by the National Council of Architectural Registration Boards (NCARB)

4. Completion of state administered Nebraska Engineers and Architects Regulation Act.

To find more information on licensing requirements visit http://www.ea.ne.gov

NEVADA:

The licensing requirements for Nevada follow a more traditional approach of requiring a professional degree, completion of the Internship Development Program (IDP) and completion of the Architect Registration Exams (ARE), but with the added requirement of a state exam and interview.

Candidates can also begin taking the ARE's before they have completed the Internship Development Program, which helps to save some time.

How to become an Architect in Nevada:

1. Complete a professional degree (B.Arch, M.Arch, D.Arch) from a National Architectural Accrediting Board (NAAB) accredited University.

2. Completion of Intern Development Program (IDP) as administered by the National Council of Architectural Registration Boards (NCARB)

3. Successful completion of Architect Registration Exam (ARE) as administered by the National Council of Architectural Registration Boards (NCARB)

4. Completion of state administered Jurisprudence Exam

5. Completion of interview

To find more information on licensing requirements visit http://www.nsbaidrd.state.nv.us/

NEW HAMPSHIRE:
The licensing requirements for New Hampshire allow for various degree paths, require completion of the Internship Development Program (IDP) and completion of the Architect Registration Exams (ARE).

Candidates can also begin taking the ARE's before they have completed the Internship Development Program, which helps to save some time.

How to become an Architect in New Hampshire:

1. Complete a professional degree (B.Arch, M.Arch, D.Arch) from a National Architectural Accrediting Board (NAAB) accredited University, or a four-year degree plus 7 years of professional experience, or 13 years of professional experience only.

2. Completion of Intern Development Program (IDP) as administered by the National Council of Architectural Registration Boards (NCARB)

3. Successful completion of Architect Registration Exam (ARE) as administered by the National Council of Architectural Registration Boards (NCARB)

To find more information on licensing requirements visit http://www.nh.gov/jtboard/arch.htm

NEW JERSEY:
The licensing requirements for New Jersey follow a more traditional approach with a little more flexibility in the experience requirement. They still require a professional degree, completion of 3 years experience and completion of the Architect Registration Exams (ARE).

How to become an Architect in New Jersey:

1. Complete a professional degree (B.Arch, M.Arch, D.Arch) from a National Architectural Accrediting Board (NAAB) accredited University.

2. Completion of three (3) calendar years of professional experience

3. Successful completion of Architect Registration Exam (ARE) as administered by the National Council of Architectural Registration Boards (NCARB)

To find more information on licensing requirements visit http://www.njconsumeraffairs.gov/arch/

NEW MEXICO:

The licensing requirements for New Mexico follow a more traditional approach of requiring a professional degree, completion of the Internship Development Program (IDP) and completion of the Architect Registration Exams (ARE).

Candidates can also begin taking the ARE's before they have completed the Internship Development Program, which helps to save some time.

How to become an Architect in New Mexico:

1. Complete a professional degree (B.Arch, M.Arch, D.Arch) from a National Architectural Accrediting Board (NAAB) accredited University.

2. Completion of Intern Development Program (IDP) as administered by the National Council of Architectural Registration Boards (NCARB)

3. Successful completion of Architect Registration Exam (ARE) as administered by the National Council of Architectural Registration Boards (NCARB)

To find more information on licensing requirements visit http://www.nmbea.org

NEW YORK:
The licensing requirements for New York allow for various education and experience possibilities and completion of the Architect Registration Exams (ARE).

How to become an Architect in New York:

1. Complete a combination of education and experience for at least 12 units which include professional and non-professional degrees, and anywhere from 5-12 years of professional experience.
For more information of units, visit http://www.op.nysed.gov/prof/arch/archlic.htm.

3. Successful completion of Architect Registration Exam (ARE) as administered by the National Council of Architectural Registration Boards (NCARB)

To find more information on licensing requirements visit http://www.op.nysed.gov/prof/arch/

NORTH CAROLINA:
The licensing requirement for North Carolina follows the traditional approach of requiring a professional degree, but do not require the completion of the Internship Development Program (IDP), and still requires the completion of the Architect Registration Exams (ARE).

Candidates can also begin taking the ARE's before they have completed the Internship Development Program, which helps to save some time.

How to become an Architect in South Carolina:

1. Complete a professional degree (B.Arch, M.Arch, D.Arch) from a National Architectural Accrediting Board (NAAB) accredited University.

2. Completion of three (3) years of experience under a registered Architect

3. Successful completion of Architect Registration Exam (ARE) as administered by the National Council of Architectural Registration Boards (NCARB)

To find more information on licensing requirements visit "http://www.ncbarch.org

NORTH DAKOTA:
The licensing requirements for North Dakota follow a more traditional approach of requiring a professional degree, completion of the Internship Development Program (IDP) and completion of the Architect Registration Exams (ARE).

Candidates can also begin taking the ARE's before they have completed the Internship Development Program, which helps to save some time.

How to become an Architect in North Dakota:

1. Complete a professional degree (B.Arch, M.Arch, D.Arch) from a National Architectural Accrediting Board (NAAB) accredited University.

2. Completion of Intern Development Program (IDP) as administered by the National Council of Architectural Registration Boards (NCARB)

3. Successful completion of Architect Registration Exam (ARE) as administered by the National Council of Architectural Registration Boards (NCARB)

To find more information on licensing requirements visit http://www.ndsba.net

OHIO:

The licensing requirements for Ohio follow a more traditional approach of requiring a professional degree, completion of the Internship Development Program (IDP) and completion of the Architect Registration Exams (ARE).

Candidates can also begin taking the ARE's before they have completed the Internship Development Program, which helps to save some time.

How to become an Architect in Ohio:

1. Complete a professional degree (B.Arch, M.Arch, D.Arch) from a National Architectural Accrediting Board (NAAB) accredited University.

2. Completion of Intern Development Program (IDP) as administered by the National Council of Architectural Registration Boards (NCARB)

3. Successful completion of Architect Registration Exam (ARE) as administered by the National Council of Architectural Registration Boards (NCARB)

To find more information on licensing requirements visit http://www.arc.ohio.gov

OKLAHOMA:

The licensing requirements for Oklahoma allow for various degree paths, require completion of the Internship Development Program (IDP) and completion of the Architect Registration Exams (ARE), and additional state exam.

Candidates can also begin taking the ARE's before they have completed the Internship Development Program, which helps to save some time.

How to become an Architect in Oklahoma:

1. Complete a professional degree (B.Arch, M.Arch, D.Arch) from a National Architectural Accrediting Board (NAAB) accredited University, or a four-year degree plus 4 years professional experience, or 10 years professional experience only.

2. Completion of Intern Development Program (IDP) as administered by the National Council of Architectural Registration Boards (NCARB)

3. Successful completion of Architect Registration Exam (ARE) as administered by the National Council of Architectural Registration Boards (NCARB)

4. Completion of state administered Acts and Rules examination.

To find more information on licensing requirements visit http://www.ok.gov/Architects

OREGON:

The licensing requirements for Oregon follow a more traditional approach of requiring a professional degree, completion of the Internship Development Program (IDP) and completion of the Architect Registration Exams (ARE), but also require an additional exam.

Candidates can also begin taking the ARE's before they have completed the Internship Development Program, which helps to save some time.

How to become an Architect in Oregon:

1. Complete a professional degree (B.Arch, M.Arch, D.Arch) from a National Architectural Accrediting Board (NAAB) accredited University.

2. Completion of Intern Development Program (IDP) as administered by the National Council of Architectural Registration Boards (NCARB)

3. Successful completion of Architect Registration Exam (ARE) as administered by the National Council of Architectural Registration Boards (NCARB)

4. Completion of State administered Jurisprudence Exam

To find more information on licensing requirements visit http://orbae.com

PENNSYLVANIA:
The licensing requirements for Pennsylvania follow a more traditional approach, which a bit more flexibility in education. They require either a professional degree, or a 4-year degree plus 6 years of experience, completion of the Internship Development Program (IDP) and completion of the Architect Registration Exams (ARE).

Candidates can also begin taking the ARE's before they have completed the Internship Development Program, which helps to save some time.

How to become an Architect in Pennsylvania:

1. Complete a professional degree (B.Arch, M.Arch, D.Arch) from a National Architectural Accrediting Board (NAAB) accredited University, or complete a 4-year degree with an additional 6 years of professional experience.

2. Completion of Intern Development Program (IDP) as administered by the National Council of Architectural Registration Boards (NCARB)

3. Successful completion of Architect Registration Exam (ARE) as administered by the National Council of Architectural Registration Boards (NCARB)

To find more information on licensing requirements visit http://www.dos.state.pa.us/portal/server.pt/community/state_architect

RHODE ISLAND:

The licensing requirements for Rhode Island follow a more traditional approach of requiring a professional degree, completion of the Internship Development Program (IDP) and completion of the Architect Registration Exams (ARE).

Candidates can also begin taking the ARE's before they have completed the Internship Development Program, which helps to save some time.

How to become an Architect in Rhode Island:

1. Complete a professional degree (B.Arch, M.Arch, D.Arch) from a National Architectural Accrediting Board (NAAB) accredited University.

2. Completion of Intern Development Program (IDP) as administered by the National Council of Architectural Registration Boards (NCARB)

3. Successful completion of Architect Registration Exam (ARE) as administered by the National Council of Architectural Registration Boards (NCARB)

To find more information on licensing requirements visit http://www.bdp.state.ri.us/architects/

SOUTH CAROLINA:
The licensing requirements for South Carolina follow a more traditional approach of requiring a professional degree, completion of the Internship Development Program (IDP) and completion of the Architect Registration Exams (ARE).

Candidates can also begin taking the ARE's before they have completed the Internship Development Program, which helps to save some time.

How to become an Architect in South Carolina:

1. Complete a professional degree (B.Arch, M.Arch, D.Arch) from a National Architectural Accrediting Board (NAAB) accredited University.

2. Completion of Intern Development Program (IDP) as administered by the National Council of Architectural Registration Boards (NCARB)

3. Successful completion of Architect Registration Exam (ARE) as administered by the National Council of Architectural Registration Boards (NCARB)

To find more information on licensing requirements visit http://www.llr.state.sc.us/pol/architects

SOUTH DAKOTA:

The licensing requirements for South Dakota follow a more traditional approach of requiring a professional degree, completion of the Internship Development Program (IDP) and completion of the Architect Registration Exams (ARE), and an additional state exam.

Candidates can also begin taking the ARE's before they have completed the Internship Development Program, which helps to save some time.

How to become an Architect in South Dakota:

1. Complete a professional degree (B.Arch, M.Arch, D.Arch) from a National Architectural Accrediting Board (NAAB) accredited University.

2. Completion of Intern Development Program (IDP) as administered by the National Council of Architectural Registration Boards (NCARB)

3. Successful completion of Architect Registration Exam (ARE) as administered by the National Council of Architectural Registration Boards (NCARB)

To find more information on licensing requirements visit http://www.dlr.sd.gov/bdcomm/btp/default.aspx

TENNESSEE:
The licensing requirements for Tennessee allow for different degree paths, completion of 3 years of experience and completion of the Architect Registration Exams (ARE).

Candidates can also begin taking the ARE's before they have completed the Internship Development Program, which helps to save some time.

How to become an Architect in Tennessee:

1. Complete a professional degree (B.Arch, M.Arch, D.Arch) from a National Architectural Accrediting Board (NAAB) accredited University, or a four-year degree plus 5 years of professional experience.

2. Completion of 3 years of professional experience

3. Successful completion of Architect Registration Exam (ARE) as administered by the National Council of Architectural Registration Boards (NCARB)

To find more information on licensing requirements visit http://www.tn.gov/regboards/ae/index.shtml

TEXAS:

The licensing requirements for Texas follow a more traditional approach of requiring a professional degree, completion of the Internship Development Program (IDP) and completion of the Architect Registration Exams (ARE).

Candidates can also begin taking the ARE's before they have completed the Internship Development Program, which helps to save some time.

How to become an Architect in Texas:

1. Complete a professional degree (B.Arch, M.Arch, D.Arch) from a National Architectural Accrediting Board (NAAB) accredited University.

2. Completion of Intern Development Program (IDP) as administered by the National Council of Architectural Registration Boards (NCARB)

3. Successful completion of Architect Registration Exam (ARE) as administered by the National Council of Architectural Registration Boards (NCARB)

To find more information on licensing requirements visit http://www.tbae.state.tx.us

UTAH:

The licensing requirements for Utah follow a more traditional approach of requiring a professional degree, completion of the Internship Development Program (IDP) and completion of the Architect Registration Exams (ARE).

Candidates can also begin taking the ARE's before they have completed the Internship Development Program, which helps to save some time.

How to become an Architect in Utah:

1. Complete a professional degree (B.Arch, M.Arch, D.Arch) from a National Architectural Accrediting Board (NAAB) accredited University.

2. Completion of Intern Development Program (IDP) as administered by the National Council of Architectural Registration Boards (NCARB)

3. Successful completion of Architect Registration Exam (ARE) as administered by the National Council of Architectural Registration Boards (NCARB)

To find more information on licensing requirements visit http://www.dopl.utah.gov

VERMONT:

The licensing requirements for Vermont allow for various degree paths, require completion of the Internship Development Program (IDP) and completion of the Architect Registration Exams (ARE).

Candidates can also begin taking the ARE's before they have completed the Internship Development Program, which helps to save some time.

How to become an Architect in Vermont:

1. Complete a professional degree (B.Arch, M.Arch, D.Arch) from a National Architectural Accrediting Board (NAAB) accredited University, or completion of a four-year degree plus 6 years of professional experience.

2. Completion of Intern Development Program (IDP) as administered by the National Council of Architectural Registration Boards (NCARB)

3. Successful completion of Architect Registration Exam (ARE) as administered by the National Council of Architectural Registration Boards (NCARB)

To find more information on licensing requirements visit http://www.vtprofessionals.org/opr1/architects/

VIRGINIA:
The licensing requirements for Virginia follow a more tradition-al approach with some exceptions for internship. They require a professional degree, completion of the Internship Develop-ment Program (IDP) and completion of the Architect Registra-tion Exams (ARE).

Candidates can also begin taking the ARE's before they have completed the Internship Development Program, which helps to save some time.

How to become an Architect in Virginia:

1. Complete a professional degree (B.Arch, M.Arch, D.Arch) from a National Architectural Accrediting Board (NAAB) ac-credited University.

2. If you complete your Internship Development Program (IDP) hours in under three years, your completion alone will qualify, otherwise you will still be held to the three (3) years of experi-ence, of which 12 months were under a registered Architect requirement.

3. Successful completion of Architect Registration Exam (ARE) as administered by the National Council of Architectural Reg-istration Boards (NCARB)

To find more information on licensing requirements visit http:// www.dpor.virginia.gov/Boards/APELS

WASHINGTON:
The licensing requirements for Washington allow for variuos degree paths, and require completion of the Internship Development Program (IDP) and completion of the Architect Registration Exams (ARE), as well as an interview.

Candidates can also begin taking the ARE's before they have completed the Internship Development Program, which helps to save some time.

How to become an Architect in Washington:

1. Complete a professional degree (B.Arch, M.Arch, D.Arch) from a National Architectural Accrediting Board (NAAB) accredited University or four-year degree plus 2 years professional experience and completion of IDP, or 6 years of professional experience only and completion of IDP.

2. Completion of Intern Development Program (IDP) as administered by the National Council of Architectural Registration Boards (NCARB)

3. Successful completion of Architect Registration Exam (ARE) as administered by the National Council of Architectural Registration Boards (NCARB)

4. Completion of interview

To find more information on licensing requirements visit http://www.dol.wa.gov/business/architects

WEST VIRGINIA:
The licensing requirements for West Virginia follow a more traditional approach of requiring a professional degree, completion of the Internship Development Program (IDP) and completion of the Architect Registration Exams (ARE).

Candidates can also begin taking the ARE's before they have completed the Internship Development Program, which helps to save some time.

How to become an Architect in West Virginia:

1. Complete a professional degree (B.Arch, M.Arch, D.Arch) from a National Architectural Accrediting Board (NAAB) accredited University.

2. Completion of Intern Development Program (IDP) as administered by the National Council of Architectural Registration Boards (NCARB)

3. Successful completion of Architect Registration Exam (ARE) as administered by the National Council of Architectural Registration Boards (NCARB)

To find more information on licensing requirements visit http://www.wvbrdarch.org

WISCONSIN:

The licensing requirements for Wisconsin allow for various education/experience combination, but still require completion of the Internship Development Program (IDP) and completion of the Architect Registration Exams (ARE).

Candidates can also begin taking the ARE's before they have completed the Internship Development Program, which helps to save some time.

How to become an Architect in Wisconsin:

1. Complete a professional degree (B.Arch, M.Arch, D.Arch) from a National Architectural Accrediting Board (NAAB) accredited University, or a four-year degree plus 3 years professional experience, or 7 years professional experience only.

2. Successful completion of Architect Registration Exam (ARE) as administered by the National Council of Architectural Registration Boards (NCARB)

To find more information on licensing requirements visit http:// dsps.wi.gov/Licenses-Permits/Architect

WYOMING:

The licensing requirements for Wyoming follow a more traditional approach of requiring a professional degree, completion of the Internship Development Program (IDP) and completion of the Architect Registration Exams (ARE).

Candidates can also begin taking the ARE's before they have completed the Internship Development Program, which helps to save some time.

How to become an Architect in Wyoming:

1. Complete a professional degree (B.Arch, M.Arch, D.Arch) from a National Architectural Accrediting Board (NAAB) accredited University.

2. Completion of Intern Development Program (IDP) as administered by the National Council of Architectural Registration Boards (NCARB)

3. Successful completion of Architect Registration Exam (ARE) as administered by the National Council of Architectural Registration Boards (NCARB)

To find more information on licensing requirements visit http:// plboards.state.wy.us/architecture

Made in the
USA
Columbia, SC